Selected Poems

Other Titles by Vernon L. Anley

A Carnival of Lies
An Unholy Love
A Divided Universe
It Happened in Hanoi
The Orange Tree and Other Stories
The Last Song

Selected Poems

Vernon L. Anley

RESOURCE *Publications* • Eugene, Oregon

SELECTED POEMS

Copyright © 2021 Vernon L. Anley. All rights reserved. Except for brief quotations in critical publications or reviews, no part of this book may be reproduced in any manner without prior written permission from the publisher. Write: Permissions, Wipf and Stock Publishers, 199 W. 8th Ave., Suite 3, Eugene, OR 97401.

Resource Publications
An Imprint of Wipf and Stock Publishers
199 W. 8th Ave., Suite 3
Eugene, OR 97401

www.wipfandstock.com

PAPERBACK ISBN: 978-1-6667-1896-6
HARDCOVER ISBN: 978-1-6667-1897-3
EBOOK ISBN: 978-1-6667-1898-0

08/06/21

Contents

Why in Such Spiritless Times | 1
How Does a Poem Come to Be | 2
Exposed to the Awesome and Mysterious | 3
The Dream Goes On for Ever | 5
Be Quiet | 6
Bombs are Falling | 7
Raise Their Souls Gently | 8
The Spirit | 9
The Dead Do Not Awaken | 10
You Turn Away | 11
We Live In Two Worlds | 12
Peace I Leave With You | 13
In Revelations | 14
A Sidelong Glance | 15
Mr. Wittgenstein | 16
Sweet Days of Breaking Light | 18
Seurat Has Unrolled His Canvas | 19
The Russians Have Developed | 21
Inspiration, Like the Johannine Pneuma | 23
Without Knowing Why | 24
In The Gospel Of Thomas | 25
Australia Is Waiting For the Poet | 26
Matisse | 27
Mr. Terrorist | 28
They Rounded a Corner | 29
One Dark Night | 30
Clouds Are Rolling Like Waves over the Criou | 31

Look How He Comes toward Us | 32
Stirred By the Sole Suggestion of a Breeze | 33
It Is Not the Sunset's Crimson Gold | 34
Kur-ing-gai | 35
We're Having a Party | 36
To the Moon | 37
I Went Out from Myself | 38
It Is a Far Reach | 39
Mystical Poems Are Utterances of Love | 40
La guitarra | 41
We Who Live On the Edge of Things | 42
Romeo and Juliet | 43
Something Must Become Of This | 44
What Seekest Thou? | 45
Would That My Heart Take Heed | 46
You May Remember Me from Time to Time | 47
Keates and Wordsworth | 48

Why in Such Spiritless Times

Who shall I tell my sorrow
my horror greener than ice.*

Why in such spiritless times
Be a poet at all?
Angels look on aghast
At what they see
A world distraught by suffering and sorrow
Soon all of us will sleep under the earth
We who never let each other sleep above it
Why linger, then
Than live and not know
What to being or to utter.

*The Russian poet Marina Tsvetayeva hanged herself out of despair.

How Does a Poem Come to Be

Some kind of feeling now within myself
Should be commencing...

—Rilke

How does a poem come to be?
From imagination and dream
And feeling things silently.
Through inwardness and though outwardness
A poem comes to be.

Exposed to the Awesome and Mysterious

Truly the gods have not revealed to mortals all things from the beginning, but by long seeking do men discover what is better.
—Xenophanes

Exposed to the awesome and mysterious
The Greeks turned to the Olympians
Aphrodite and Zeus, owl-eyed Athena
And Artemis, the goddess with a hundred breasts
For the meaning of life.

The lords of Olympus,
Emancipated from ordinary existence
Were brought to earth
By man's knowledge of his spiritual nature
And his transcendence over nature.

Detached from divine meddling
The Olympians took refuge in the arts:
In the plays of Aeschylus and Euripides
The poetry of Pindar
In music and sculpture.

We have our own Olympians
Priestly inventions
Risen from the dead
To a heavenly mode of being
With access to God

Sustained by worship and ritual
Our immortals live on
In the holy of holies
Proclaiming salvation for all
And eternal life.

The Greeks dismissed their Gods
But their protégées live on.
Secure in man's need of image and myth
That symbolize his orientation
To the known unknown.

The Dream Goes On for Ever

The mystic death is the beginning of eternal life.
—Jacob Boehme

The dream goes on for ever
Only the dreamers die
Past reason's last endeavour
Belief's lost ecstasy

Be Quiet

Be quiet
The young girl said
Can't you see
I'm listening to the Orange Tree
"I hear no voice,"
It's an enchanted tree, the young girl said
A light not of the sky
Lives in the Orange Tree
"I see no light"
You do not see what I see
Let me be
So I may listen to the Orange Tree
"I hear no voice"
There is no voice, the young girl said
But it is almost sound
And it falls from the Orange Tree
"What does it say I asked"
It tells of a time when the world was happy
And man could do no wrong
Animals had learned to speak
And birds sing songs for him
"I hear no voice and see no light"
Your heart is empty
The young girl said
Without love you will not see
What I can see
The light that lives in the Orange Tree.

Bombs are Falling

The War in Syria.

Bombs are falling
The dead lie buried beneath the rubble
A woman screams
Her child recognized
By the ring on her finger
She falls to the ground
She beseeches God
'Why? What for?'
But the heavens are silent,
The pilot smiles
God's sorrow
Lies hidden
In the woman's heart.

Raise Their Souls Gently

They asked not for birth
Nor for life
Nor for this world
With its history of suffering
You offer beauty
The natural world and starry skies
But beauty fadeth like the flower
You offer love
To assuage their loneliness
But love is fickle
And perishes with the body.
There are tears in the heart of reality.
'Why, O God, maketh thou man?
For what purpose?'

The Spirit

The Spirit
That breaks every bud to flower
Has called me to its side
Day hears it not, nor night
Nor minaret, dome, or spire
But in the silence of my heart
It speaks my name.

The Dead Do Not Awaken

The dead do not awaken
To their mother's arms
To family portraits
The embrace of friends

The soldier boy
Makes nought of these
But gives his life
To gunfire and death

To have loved and die is life
To forego love for death
Is life's loss
And death's victory.

You Turn Away

You turn away
Showing your disgust
At my unkempt hair
My ragged clothes
My broken nails

Your pretty dress
Your pearl earrings
Hide what you are
What I am
What we are.

When death takes us
Between silk sheets
Or alleyways
With blessings
Or without

We will know ourselves
As we are
Not 'I' not 'You'
But one in being
In spirit and in love.

We Live In Two Worlds

We live in two worlds: the world of daily life that operates in standard time and standard space, and the world of our imagination.
—Max Weber

The Daoist teacher Chuang Tzu
Dreamt he was a butterfly
Flitting and fluttering about
Happily doing as he pleased.
He didn't know if he was Chuang Tzu
For he was in a different reality.
He woke up suddenly
And there he was
In his body
Solid and unmistakable Chuang Tzu.
But he didn't know if he was Chuang Tzu
Who dreamt he was a butterfly
Or a butterfly
Dreaming he was Chaung Tzu

Peace I Leave With You

The dead shall live
Their bodies rise

—Isaiah

Peace I leave with you
My peace I give you
Do not let your heart
Be troubled

I have called you by your name
You are mine
Neither darkness nor death
Will stand in your way

I am your salivation
And you shall know my love
And abideth with me
For all eternity

Absolutely unmagical!
Unmythical, unspeculative even
A divine self-bestowal and alliance of love
That brings man to God.

In Revelations

After this life God himself is our place.
—Saint Augustine

In Revelations
The hymnic language is high flown
Suggesting
Exciting possibilities
In the heavenly world.

And God shall wipe away all tears from their eyes;
and there shall be no more death, neither sorrow,
nor crying, neither shall there be any more pain

Every man enters the world with a cry
Yet their is cause to rejoice
There is no place for suffering
In the messianic kingdom
Not even for death.

Most assuredly, I tell you, hereafter you will see heaven

A Sidelong Glance

A sidelong glance
Who has not known it?
When something
More than appearance
Passes between you
The whole heart's movement
In one passing glance
Too fleeting to hold
Too ephemeral to know.

Mr. Wittgenstein

What can be said at all can be said clearly: and whereof one cannot speak thereof one must be silent.

—Ludwig Wittgenstein

Mr. Wittgenstein

Have you never been in love?
Have you always found the words
To say what you feel
When your heart
Soars above the world
And you experience a joy
You never imagined
Or expected to find.

Mr. Wittgenstein

Have you never
Come face to face with beauty?
Have you never felt
The quickening stillness
When your spirit
Engages with beauty
Freeing itself
From time and space.

Mr. Wittgenstein

Have you never gazed into the night sky
Ablaze with stars
And felt an unseen something
A *mysterium magnum*
Sweeping through the universe
Enlivening earth's myriad forms
Filling your heart
With wonder and awe.

Mr. Wittgenstein

Rational truths
And unequivocal statements.
Belong to perishable facts
Of to the physical world
They ignore the joys of the spirit
And the gifts of the heart.

Ah, what a dusty answer gets the soul
When out for certainties in this life.

So you see Mr. Wittgenstein
Besides the gifts of the head,
There are those of the heart
Emotional experiences
Brought to life by feelings
That we do nothing to arrange
But which give meaning to our lives.

Sweet Days of Breaking Light

Sweet days of breaking light!
The trees are aflame with Autumn!
A voiceless tide of falling leaves
Floods the air with gold.
Joy spreads through flowers and colours
Expanding through the visible whole of beauty
Till heart and dream become as one
Soli Deo gloria!

Seurat Has Unrolled His Canvas

'A Sunday on La Grande Jatte'
—1884 Georges Seurat

Seurat has unrolled his canvas
In Russell Square
Allowing the Parisians,
To step out of the painting
And join us.

You must admit it's a beautiful day
The sky is an unbroken curve of stainless blue
And the mid-afternoon sunlight
Bathes the park in a celestial mid-afternoon glow

You would expect Seurat's Parisians
To talk and smile and gesture at things
That catch their attention
Or, at the very least, to show some engagement
With their surroundings as they congregate
To enjoy a sunny afternoon.

But the impression, you will agree
Is one of absolute stillness
As if time had lost meaning
And become frozen
Take the fashionable couple with the dog.

The man, elegantly dressed
In top hat and silk cravat
Is as motionless as a figure on a marble frieze
And his wife, certainly a *femme de mode*
In her stylish coat and fur collar
Is equally still and silent.

Seurat has us see our companions
As strangers to themselves and each other
Inhabiting a world that is not rightly theirs
And to which they do not belong.
And what of us?

Are we like Seurat's wealthy Parisians
Mute players in the drama of living?
The setting is beautiful
The lighting superb
The costumes gorgeous
But wherefore the play?

The Russians Have Developed

I looked at the earth, and it was empty and nothing,
—Jer 4:23

The Russians have developed
A hypersonic missile as fast a bullet
The Americans, not to be outdone
Are making a super hypersonic missile
And the Chinese
In keeping with their ambition
To be masters of the world
Are developing a missile
In every way superior
To the Russian and American missiles.

The end, if anyone is in doubt,
Is a corpse strewn world
Of Russian, American and Chinese bodies
Not to mention ourselves
Blasted to death by atomic missiles
Nor will the earth escape destruction.
But become another knot
In the string of dead planets around the sun.

If you carry on Mr. President
Say good-by to your wife and children
To the air that you breathe
To your dacha in the woods
The pride that sustained your glory
And pray that the Spirit
That holdeth our souls in life
Will forgive you.

Inspiration, Like the Johannine Pneuma

Inspiration, like the Johannine *pneuma*
Blows where it will
You do not know from whence it comes
Or where it goes
Which is why Rodin told Rilke
Not to wait for the word
That brings verse to the pen
But to work tirelessly
With what memory recollects
And the eye can see.

Inspiration dwells at ease
In the soul of the genius
Asking neither for divine guidance
Nor remembered emotion
But we who labour

Bound by a vaguely-felt necessity
Must wait for the word
To what will become known
In verse and in rhyme.

Without Knowing Why

Without knowing why
A sudden something
An image caught in passing
A phrase of music
Recalls a time
When happiness was joy
And love
The only thing we knew.

In The Gospel Of Thomas

In the Gospel of Thomas
A disciple asks Jesus
'Tell us about our end. What will it be?'
anticipating a glorious resurrection.
But Jesus is no mystagogue
He denies the disciple fetching images of well being
And replies, *'Have you found the Beginning,*
so that now you seek the end? The place of the beginning,
will be the place of the end.'
Shaken by Jesus' rebuke
That God is *Alpha and Omega*
And that only the eternal
Can give meaning to the temporal
The disciple was brought to see
That Jesus was not a rabbi (as Nicodemus proposed)
But the Messiah
God's blessed Son and emissary.

Australia Is Waiting For the Poet

Australia is waiting for the poet
To paint in words
The landscape of its artists
The excessive spaces
And timeless waves of being
That sweep across the Outback
The parched ochre of ancient flood plains.
Where local spirits laid songlines
And the souls geographer brought dreaming
To a land laid bare by time

Matisse

I took fright, realizing that I could not turn back, so I went ahead, urged forward by I know not what—a force that is quite alien to my normal life as a man.

—Matisse

/ɪnspɪˈreɪʃ(ə)n/, *inspirare, inspiratiuon*
A restless creative spirit that summons the artist
And make him its instrument.
There is an anonymity to this gift of the spirit.
Like the Johannine *pneuma* it blows where it wills
You hear the sound of it
But you do not know from whence it came
Or where it is going.
In itself it is wordless and imageless
An intuition striving for expression
Freeing creativity from the occasional and transitory
Into the realm of the enduring.

Mr. Terrorist

The spirit of God hath made me, and the breath of the Almighty hath given me life.

—JOB 33:4

Mr. Terrorist
Do you know who you are?
Do you know who we are?
Do you know who I am?

The gun you put to my head
Will blow me apart
But what you kill
Is not a spiritless body
What you kill is a living soul
That makes you
That make me
A thing apart
A bearer of God's own spirit.

You are not listening
Mr. Terrorist
You will not listen
You cannot listen
Because you are one of those
You think we are
A soulless body
Without spirit.

They Rounded a Corner

Se volvieron a encontrar
al revolver una esquina
Y como dos criaturas
Se pusieron a llorar.
El amor no tiene cura.

—Cante Flamenco

They rounded a corner
And met again
And like two children
Began to cry.
Love has no cure.

One Dark Night

One dark night
With no other light or guide
Than the one that burned in my heart
I went out unseen
To where he waited for me
Wholly taken by love
I abandoned and forgot myself
Leaving my caress
Forgotten among the lilies.

Clouds Are Rolling Like Waves over the Criou

Clouds are rolling like waves over the *Criou*,
When the storm breaks
Shoppers will shelter in the *Bar de Savoie*
Behind beaded curtains
And mad dog Toto
Whose only happiness is barking at strangers
Will run indoors.

When the rain stops
The clouds over the *Criou*
Will be forgotten
The sky will clear
And people will go about their business
In the *Place du Gros-Tilleul*
And Toto, always watchful
Will bark again.

All that holds the memory
Of the clouds rolling over the *Criou*
The bar with the beaded curtains
The shoppers in the *Gros-Tilleul*
And mad dog Toto
From being forgotten
Are these lines of verse uttered in passing.

Look How He Comes Toward Us

Look how he comes toward us
Through the flowering grass
And slowly
A song on his lips
His heart open
To things that are visible and invisible.
That he is now one of those who know,
Need it be told?

Stirred By the Sole Suggestion of a Breeze

Stirred by the sole suggestion of a breeze
The artist's water garden at Giverny
Mirrors with reflective ease
The floating colours of autumn

The poet would paint the garden as Monet saw it
In blues and greens, the coloured banks of flowers
Admired by Cezanne and Caillebotte
Mingled in one dream of light.

But rhyme is far afield from heaven's brush
To paint autumn's golden hour
When hearts of flowers on the air are borne
And colours reveal the artist's dream.

It Is Not the Sunset's Crimson Gold

It is not the sunset's crimson gold
Or the horizon's burning fire
that awakens my sleeping dreams
But sweet darkness and the moon's velvet glow
That quickens the timeless hours
When breast is joined to breast
And night, its spread wings rustling
Folds us among the stars.

Kur-ing-gai

Kur-ing-gai
Home of the Kuringai people
Whose paintings and songlines
Trace the path of Creator-Beings
Who sang the world into existence
And made every thing beautiful.

Born of a knowledge from within
For he set the world in their hearts
They divine God's nature
Through the revelation of his works
Made visible to the eye of the human soul.

We who would give our all
To bear witness to the creation of the world
Must wait for the appointed time
When the invisible things of *Him*
From the creation of the world are seen
Are understood by the things that are made.

We're Having a Party

I don't believe in God, I turn my back
On thought, and as for that old irony called love
I want to hear no more of that again.

—Paul Verlaine

We're having a party
Oh Yeah!
Bring your machine guns and your machetes
We're having a party
Oh Yeah!
We're going on a killing spree
Compassion is for the dogs
Oh Yeah!
We're having a party!
The dead fall in moaning heaps!
The more the merrier!
Oh Yeah!
The God Shiva
Has appeared in our midst
Dancing the world to pieces !
Oh Yeah!

To the Moon

To the moon
And onwards to Mars
And the heavens beyond
And this is just the beginning:
Marvellous are the works of man

But our place
Is not the stars
Or other worlds
But a spiritual flight
Into heaven's glory

Death takes us
Beyond all endeavour
Unveiled and perfected
Into the finality
Of eternity itself.

I Went Out from Myself

I went out from myself
Leaving my cares
Forgotten among the lilies

How blissful to walk
In the shadow of saints
The heart beguiled
By spiritual feelings
So delicate and delightful
That the soul communes
Inwardly with God.

It Is a Far Reach

It is a far reach
From here to eternity
Beyond the farthest shore
And distant horizon
And then the voyaging has just begun

When the soul's last breath
Brings life to an end
We hear tell of irrepressible sighs
And mystical visions
That no man can imagine.

We who know not tomorrow
Cannot know the unknowable
Must wait for death
To bring to light
The hidden things of darkness

Mystical Poems Are Utterances of Love

Mystical poems are utterances of love
A breath of pure spirit
Spoken with delicate sweetness
From the depth of the soul

We share the intuition
Of something more to be known
A presence inexpressible
That holds us in being

Poets write of love and beauty
And pain and pleasure
Where the same transcendent spirit
Makes itself felt

And leave to the mystic
The mystery of his union
At the intersection
Of the timeless with time

La guitarra

La guitarra
desgrans notas
que son garras
en penas remotas.

You draw notes from the guitar that fall like arrows
on pains I'd forgotten.

We Who Live On the Edge of Things

We painters can never reproduce sunlight as it really is. I can only approach the truth of it.

—Joaquin Scrolla

We who live on the edge of things
Are too full of our own beginning
To see reality as it really is
We only see the shape of things
Their appearance
Their passing

Were we to see
The hidden life of things
All would be one in *Being*
Sustained by the Spirit
That calls the stars its own
And we by name

Romeo and Juliet

Our young lovers
Overwhelmed by romance
Imagined that love
Would raise them entwined
Into paradise
Where youth keeps its innocence
And beauty its complexion.

Alas, only the gods
Retain their appearance
Their spirits clothed in human form
We mortals
Deprived of resurrection
Must suffer the ignominy
Of disappearance and death.

Our salvation
Lies within life's embrace
Whether broken or lost
Love will regain its composure
And find its place in our lives
Without supplication
Or heaven's endeavour.

Something Must Become Of This

I was set up from everlasting, from the beginning, before the earth was.
—Proverbs 8:23

If the eye could match the soul's vision
It would see the invisible things of him
From the creation of the heavens
To the end of the world
When all will become known.

What Seekest Thou?

'What seekest thou?'
Prospero asked Miranda (his angelic daughter)
For in paradise we see things
In a state of ethereal beauty
And perfectly transparent.
But Prospero, having a physical body
Whose magic powers
Were subject to natural law
Was denied the sight of invisible things:
For the invisible things of heaven
From the creation of the world
Are not seen by the things that are made.

Would That My Heart Take Heed

Think you 'midst this might sum
Of things for ever speaking
That nothing of itself will come
But we must still be seeking.

—Wordsworth

Would that my heart take heed
Of nature's voiceless whispers
That bid my heart
Be still and rest:
Seek not, and think not;
Dream, and know not;
This is best.

You May Remember Me from Time to Time

You may remember me from time to time
Walking together as once we did
Arm in arm
Talking of inconsequential things
You may remember the scene:
The woodland path set among chestnut trees
The lake with its picturesque boat house
And the grey green hills beneath floating clouds

You may remember me from time to time
But then again, you may not
A fleeting memory
Caught between daylight and dream
Walking together as once we did.
Arm in arm among the chestnut trees
Beside the picturesque boat house
And in the distance
Silent hills against the sky.

Keates and Wordsworth

Keates and Wordsworth
And other great poets
Speak to us from natural necessity
In words that reveal
The spiritual activity behind reality
But we whose sensibilities are tied to the visible world
And whose hearts reflects our own pursuits
Can take comfort from Theocritus' words
To the young poet Eumenes
Who after struggling for two years
Managed to write only one idyll:

And if you are on the first step
you ought to be proud and pleased
Coming as far as this is not little;
what you have achieved deserves great praise.
For even this first step
is far distant from the common lot.
To set your foot upon this step
you must rightfully be a citizen
of the city of ideas.
And in that city it is hard
and rare to be naturalized.
Coming as far this is not little.
What you have achieved is great glory

www.ingramcontent.com/pod-product-compliance
Lightning Source LLC
Chambersburg PA
CBHW072037060426
42449CB00010BA/2304